DATE DUE		

**796.44
LAW**

3 24891 0901257 2
Lawrence, Blythe.

Girls' gymnastics

**PEIRCE ES
CHICAGO PUBLIC SCHOOLS**

Girls'
GYMNASTICS

by Blythe Lawrence

GIRLS'

SportsZone

Published by ABDO Publishing Company, PO Box 398166, Minneapolis, MN 55439. Copyright © 2014 by Abdo Consulting Group, Inc. International copyrights reserved in all countries. No part of this book may be reproduced in any form without written permission from the publisher. SportsZone™ is a trademark and logo of ABDO Publishing Company.

Printed in the United States of America,
North Mankato, Minnesota

052013
122013

Editor: Chrös McDougall
Series Designer: Marie Tupy

Photo Credits: Serg Zastavkin/Shutterstock Images, cover, title; Julian Finney/Getty Images, 5; Matt Dunham/AP Images, 7, 9; Amy Sancetta/AP Images, 10; The Yomiuri Shimbun/AP Images, 13; Koji Sasahara/AP Images, 15; Bullit Marquez/AP Images, 17; Jeff Roberson/AP Images, 18; Kathy Willens/ AP Images, 21, 23; Al Tielemans/Sports Illustrated/Getty Images, 25, 26; Jamie Squire/Getty Images, 29; Julie Jacobson/AP Images, 31, 32, 34, 42; Gregory Bull/AP Images, 37, 40; Thomas Coex/AFP/ Getty Images, 39; Red Line Editorial, Inc., 44

Library of Congress Control Number: 2013932514

Cataloging-in-Publication Data

Lawrence, Blythe.
 Girls' gymnastics / Blythe Lawrence.
   p. cm. -- (Girls' sportszone)
 ISBN 978-1-61783-986-3 (lib. bdg.)
 Includes bibliographical references and index.
 1. Gymnastics for girls--Juvenile literature.   I. Title.
 796.44--dc23

                                                     2013932514

GIRLS' SportsZone

chapter 1

Power and Grace with Shawn Johnson and Nastia Liukin

Nastia Liukin and Shawn Johnson stood side by side on the podium at the 2008 Olympic Games in Beijing, China. They waved to the crowd and beamed as the American anthem played. As the stars of the strong US women's gymnastics team, they were both tough and fierce. But as gymnasts, they had little else in common.

Liukin was the artistic one. At 5 feet, 3 inches, she was fairly tall for an elite gymnast. That gave her a graceful, elegant look on each gymnastics event. Liukin's grace came from her mom, who had been a world champion rhythmic gymnast for the Soviet Union.

Liukin's father was a two-time Olympic gold medalist for the Soviet Union in men's gymnastics. He had been known more for his power

Shawn Johnson, *left*, and Nastia Liukin, *center*, stand on the medal podium at the 2008 Olympic Games.

A NOTE ON JUDGING

Beginning in 2006, judges began giving not one but two scores for each routine. The difficulty score measures how hard the skills in the routine are. It is sometimes called the D-score. Gymnasts get extra points for doing difficult moves in combination with one another. The execution score (E-score) is based on form. A separate panel of judges calculates this score. Execution judges start from 10 points and deduct tenths of a point for form errors. At the end of a routine, the D-score is added to the E-score for the total score on the event.

and strength. That was not Nastia's style, though. In fact, those characteristics better described Johnson.

Johnson was the daredevil. She was shorter, standing just 4-foot-9. She was also muscular. That helped her power through high-risk routines. Some gymnasts are so tense and focused that they show little emotion while competing. That was not Johnson. She was known for her big smile in between events.

Liukin and Johnson were two of the most popular US athletes going into the 2008 Games. Both were favored to win several medals in Beijing. But only one could win the most coveted all-around title. Women's gymnastics includes four events: vault, uneven bars, balance beam, and floor exercise. The gymnast who has the highest combined score in all four events is the all-around champion.

Indeed, the all-around competition became a battle between the two friends. Their first event was vault. As expected, Johnson took an early lead by performing a difficult 2.5 twisting Yurchenko. That was much harder than Liukin's vault, which had only 1.5 twists.

But Liukin had the advantage when they moved to uneven bars. Her routine was one of the most difficult in the world. It included many skills that demonstrated her shoulder flexibility and showcased her exceptional swing. She performed it well to take a slight lead over Johnson. Both gymnasts were almost flawless on the balance beam. Johnson used her power to get incredible height above the beam on daring acrobatic combinations. Liukin performed clever combinations of leaps, jumps, and acrobatic skills. After three events, Liukin still held a slight lead.

Shawn Johnson performs on the floor exercise during the 2008 Olympic all-around competition.

BACK TO BASICS

Most coaches agree that the best way to encourage good form in gymnastics is to go back to ballet. That dancing style is the root of gymnastics. So in addition to regular gymnastics training, many gymnasts also study ballet. Ballet helps with flexibility and movement. Ballet classes also help gymnasts polish dance skills and refine their movements. That usually leads to higher execution scores.

The competition came down to the final event, floor exercise. Liukin had the lead. But Johnson was the defending world champion. She was also known for her better tumbling skills. Liukin's routine was less powerful. She seemed to float through the air on leaps and twists. And she gave away little in form deductions. She scored 15.525 points.

Then Johnson took the floor. The strength of her routine was difficult, high-flying tumbling passes. But Johnson had seen the scoreboard. She knew she needed a higher score than had been seen on floor during the Games to take the gold medal from Liukin. It was probably not going to happen. Nonetheless, she performed a marvelous floor routine. It was one of the best of her life. When it was over, she beamed with pride and stood looking at the scoreboard, waiting.

After several tense minutes, the scoreboard flashed 15.525, the same score as Liukin's. There was a roar of approval from the crowd inside Beijing's National Indoor Stadium. Johnson had earned the Olympic silver medal. Liukin had taken gold. It was the best finish American gymnasts had ever had at an Olympic Games.

"Going into this, we knew that there could be only one champion," Johnson said later. "We're very lucky to both say that we won a medal for our country."

In the following days, each won more individual medals. Johnson got a gold on balance beam and a silver on floor. Liukin took silver on bars and beam, and bronze on floor. They left Beijing as two of the most decorated stars of the Games.

Nastia Liukin executes a release move on the uneven bars during the 2008 Olympic all-around competition.

Combining Power and Grace

Liukin and Johnson had very different strengths as gymnasts. Yet both were favorites going into the all-around competition. That is because both are excellent examples of the dual nature of gymnastics. The sport requires athletes to have both power and grace. Without some of both, neither Liukin nor Johnson would have been as successful.

Many people watching gymnastics notice the acrobatic maneuvers. These are things such as flips and twists. But dance movements such as leaps and turns are also important. Judges look for gymnasts to show good

Nastia Liukin shows her grace while performing on the balance beam during the 2008 Olympic all-around competition.

Quick Tip: Strength Builders

A gymnast looking to become more powerful on vault and floor exercise should work on increasing her strength. Due to her lanky shape, Nastia had to do just that. Nastia explains, "I never had to work as hard on flexibility and dance as I did on strength. I remember to this day spending hours and hours a day conditioning in the gym, and running and running up hills and sprints and jumps and all these things. And that's something that to a lot of the other gymnasts is second nature."

form in both areas. Examples of good form include straight legs, pointed toes, and correct technique on gymnastic movements. Gymnasts also try to make their routines look easy to do, even when they're not.

"We really put a lot of time and effort, a lot of hard work into it to make it look really easy," Liukin said.

Liukin and Johnson were best known for being either graceful or powerful. But each gymnast was actually excellent in both areas. Liukin did not have Johnson's explosive power. But she was able to do difficult tumbling passes on floor and a relatively complicated vault. Because she was short, Johnson was often unfairly criticized for not being artistic. In fact, she showed excellent form on all of her skills. She later used her artistry to help win first place on *Dancing with the Stars*.

chapter 2

Balance Beam with Jordyn Wieber

The world's top gymnasts met in Tokyo, Japan, nine months before the 2012 Olympic Games. They were there for the World Championships, an event that takes place every year when there are no Olympic Games.

Before the competition, all eyes were on two young women. Both were competing for the first time on the world's biggest stage. One was Viktoria Komova of Russia. The other was Jordyn Wieber, a rising star from Michigan.

Komova was the daughter of a very successful Soviet gymnast. The year before, she had won the Youth Olympic Games in Singapore with a stunning performance. Many favored her to win the 2011 world all-around

Jordyn Wieber performs on the balance beam during the all-around final at the 2011 World Championships.

CONQUERING FEAR

There is little room for error on the balance beam. As such, many gymnasts think beam is the most nerve-racking event. Jordyn Wieber deals with the pressure by visualizing a perfect routine. She also reminds herself of all the preparation she's done. "I call it getting into my zone before the competition," Wieber said. "A lot of times I'm just running through my keywords in my head, all the keywords that I practice in my head in the gym every single day, just making it feel totally normal."

title. Wieber was still very young. But she was known for having nerves of steel in competition. That was especially true on her best event, the balance beam.

"Her mental edge is her razor sharp focus, that ability to just block everything else out and deliver under pressure," Wieber's coach John Geddert said. "Some kids get antsy about being in the spotlight. She actually likes it."

As expected Wieber and Komova both reached the all-around finals. But Wieber made a costly mistake on bars early in the competition, and Komova moved into the lead. Wieber knew she would need to be almost perfect on balance beam to stay in the hunt for the all-around title. That was a tough assignment. On beam, the tiniest mistake can be the difference between a hit routine and one with a fall. Wieber would need to put all of her focus into this routine. It would have to be the best routine of her life.

Wieber concentrated hard as she prepared to begin her routine. In fact she said she even stopped hearing the crowd and the noises of the arena. She took a deep breath. Then she began the routine the same way she had done it a thousand times in practice.

Wieber jumped into her middle splits mount and began her routine. Most gymnasts prefer to do their toughest skills at the beginning of their beam routines. This way, they get the difficulty out of the way early. Then they can relax and focus on the rest of the routine. But not Wieber.

Jordyn Wieber leaps into the air during the all-around finals at the 2011 World Championships.

DAREDEVIL SKILLS

The most difficult salto elements on beam are those where a gymnast adds a half or full twist. Those moves are left to the extreme daredevils, however. Kennedy Baker is a member of the US National Team. She says watching others do a back flip with a full twist on beam always amazes her. "I'm just like, 'Wow,'" she said. "Gabby [Douglas] is like, 'It's so easy!' and I'm like, 'Um, OK.'"

Her routine was difficult from beginning to end. It included several complicated combinations of acrobatic skills, each one supremely difficult.

For nearly a minute and a half Wieber performed. She flipped and leaped flawlessly high above the four-inch beam. Then she landed lightly and confidently each time. Finally Wieber took a slight pause and raised herself onto her toes. She prepared herself for the most difficult skill in her routine: a standing back salto with a full twist. She swung her arms up and jumped backward into the air.

It was a high, graceful flip. From the start her shoulders were always perfectly square with the beam. That gave her plenty of opportunity while upside down to spot her landing. She was in perfect position as her feet hit the beam. And she continued the routine without the smallest wobble.

Wieber's dismount was flawless. The spectators had fallen silent during her routine. They burst into applause when she landed.

There was a hint of a smile on Wieber's face as she turned away from the beam. She knew the routine had put her back in the battle for the title. Meanwhile, Komova's beam routine was shaky. It cost her dearly. By the end of the competition, Wieber had narrowly pulled away. That helped her win her first world all-around title.

"We thought everything is lost, but Jordyn is such a strong person," a jubilant US National Team Coordinator Martha Karolyi said after the meet. "She's just somebody with real special abilities who is able to fight back as strong as she did. Most people get very disappointed and distracted by a mistake, but she didn't."

Jordyn Wieber used a strong balance beam routine to help win the 2011 world all-around championship and team title.

Finding a Balance on Beam

More than any other event, balance beam makes gymnasts nervous. The smallest mistake can lead to a fall. So a gymnast has to be careful just when walking across the beam. Imagine landing, flipping, and turning on the four-inch plank (10 cm), and making it look perfectly natural. Yet that's just what the most advanced gymnasts do.

A salto element is a move where a gymnast does a flip without touching her hands to the ground (or in this case, to the beam). Top-level

Jordyn Wieber performs a backflip while on the balance beam at the 2012 US championships in St. Louis.

Quick Tip: Start on a Line

Even after learning a salto, gymnasts need a lot of practice before they can do it on the high beam. Coach Mary Lee Tracy suggests progressing gradually. Start by working the flip on a line on the floor and pretending you're doing it on the beam. Then move to a practice beam a few inches off the ground. Practice doing the skill onto a beam-high mat with a line drawn on it to simulate the end of the beam.

gymnasts are required to have a combination of at least two flipping elements in their beam routines. This is called a "flight series." The gymnast uses the first flip to build momentum for a second and possibly a third salto.

Balance beam is about taking risks. Nothing is riskier than flipping upside down without using your hands. It takes incredible precision to turn your body over in the air and land on a four-inch plank and stay on, let alone make it look easy.

Front or back handsprings often set up elements where the gymnast flips through the air without using her hands. A gymnast may land the flip one foot at a time in what's called a walkout. Others choose to land with both feet at the same time on the beam. As with release moves on bars, judges look for good form on salto elements, including pointed toes and straight legs.

chapter 3

Uneven Bars with Gabrielle Douglas

At the end of 2012, Gabrielle "Gabby" Douglas was one of the most famous Olympians from that summer's Olympic Games. Yet at the beginning of that year, she was relatively unknown. It all began to change at the American Cup, a major gymnastics meet four months before the Olympics began.

Douglas was not an official competitor for the American Cup, though. She was added to the lineup just a week before the meet. Even then she was only an alternate. That meant her scores would not count. But in the end, they did not need to. Douglas let her gymnastics do the talking.

Gabby Douglas flies high above the bar while warming up before competing in the 2012 American Cup.

NOT JUST FOR THE SHORT GIRLS

Russia's Svetlana Khorkina stood at 5 feet, 5 inches. But she wasn't going to let being "tall" hamper her success on uneven bars. Khorkina worked with her coach, Boris Pilkin. They figured out ways to use her height to her advantage. In the process they invented several new moves that made bars easier for taller gymnasts. Khorkina's originality on all events won her the praise of the gymnastics world. However, she was always best on bars. That is where she won two Olympic gold medals (1996 and 2000) and had eight moves named after her.

She mounted the uneven bars in the second rotation. Douglas had always been a strong all-around gymnast, but she really set herself apart on the uneven bars. It was the event where she flew highest. Partway through her routine, she let go of the bar and sailed backward. Her body jackknifed through the air as she flew over the high bar. Douglas reached for the bar. For a split second, it seemed too far away. Then her hands closed around it. She continued to swing.

Focus, Douglas reminded herself as she caught the bar. She swung smoothly into her next skill. Gymnasts can stop and take a breath between skills on balance beam or floor exercise. That is not the case on the uneven bars. Halting the momentum even a little bit on the uneven bars results in a one-point deduction. That is the same amount taken away for falling off the balance beam. Douglas had come to the American Cup to make an impression. A mistake like that was not in her plans.

There had been a time when Douglas thought she wasn't good on uneven bars. But in time it became her best event. She had a natural swing and good form. But most importantly, she could achieve incredible height on her release skills. Those are moves where a gymnast lets go of the bar and then grabs it again. US National Team Coordinator Martha Karolyi is a tough judge. But she was impressed by Douglas's high-flying abilities. She even nicknamed Douglas "The Flying Squirrel."

Douglas's signature release move was a Tkatchev. That is when a gymnast lets go of the high bar, flies over it going backward, and regrabs the bar in time to swing smoothly out. Douglas's Tkatchevs always wowed

Gabby Douglas performs on the uneven bars during the 2012 American Cup.

the crowd because she flew so high.

Gymnastics fans had high hopes for the US women. They had won the world championship in 2011. Going into 2012, an Olympic team gold medal seemed within reach. There was one event in which the team sometimes struggled, however. "The uneven bars is one event where we are not quite as strong," Karolyi admitted in 2011.

Douglas and her coach Liang Chow took advantage of that. They debuted a new routine that included two Tkatchevs at the American Cup. Douglas was not part of the official competition. But the judges still gave her a score on bars that would have won first place. An even bigger surprise came at the end. Douglas had the highest all-around score as well. It was a big surprise for US gymnastics fans. After all, the American Cup featured some of the best gymnasts in the world. With just a few months before the 2012 Olympic Games, Douglas had begun to make a name for herself. "I think this is going to be a big step for me, where I really take off," she had said before the competition. She was more right than she could know. Five months later, she would be the Olympic all-around champion.

Mastering the Bars

The uneven bars is one of the most technical events in women's gymnastics. It takes precision and strength (and a lot of hard work) to master the basics of the event. But once those have been learned, a gymnast can move on to more complicated skills, including release moves.

The Tkatchev that Douglas performed is one of the more difficult release moves. It requires the gymnast to release the bar and soar backward and over it, regrasping the bar when it is about level with her chest. The Tkatchev can be done in a variety of ways. Most gymnasts learn a

Gabby Douglas celebrates with teammate Aly Raisman at the 2012 American Cup.

regular Tkatchev. That is when they straddle their legs as they go over the bar. It's also possible to do a Tkatchev in a piked position. That is where the gymnast bends at the hips but keeps her legs glued together.

There are even more advanced versions of the Tkatchev. In one, a gymnast will swing into the skill with both her hands and toes on the bar.

Gabby Douglas shows off her incredible height on a release move during the 2012 Olympic Games.

Quick Tip: Swing, Swing

Gymnasts practice a great deal before learning release moves. Coach Al Fong has a good way for gymnasts to prepare. He suggests the gymnast practice swinging from the high bar to the low bar while trying not to touch their feet on the ground. That way, the gymnast gets used to releasing a bar and catching it again without doing anything too complicated. Later, a gymnast might swing backward on high bar, let go of the bar and fly over the low bar, trying to catch the low bar as she comes down.

Using her legs and feet, she'll push off the bar to get more height and flight as she flies over it. These "toe on" skills are riskier and more difficult. But they nearly always draw roars of approval from the crowd.

The Tkatchev is one of the most popular skills on uneven bars. What separates good from great Tkatchevs is the amount of height a gymnast gets when performing the skill. Having good form is key. That means the gymnast's legs should be straight and her toes pointed. However, great height on Tkatchevs can make the judges sit up and take note.

That said, release moves are not for beginners. In fact, learning a release skill on bars is seen as something of a rite of passage to very advanced gymnastics. Asked about her proudest moment in gymnastics, two-time Olympic gold medalist Shannon Miller said: "Learning my first release move ranks right up there."

chapter 4

Vault with McKayla Maroney

The women's gymnastics team final is often one of the most anticipated events of the Olympic Games. That was certainly the case for American fans in 2012. The United States had won the women's team gold medal just once, in 1996. But many believed the 2012 squad could do it again in London, England. If they did, their dominance on vault would be a big reason. And there was one gymnast who stood above the rest on that event.

McKayla Maroney stood at the edge of the vault runway. She stared hard at the obstacle 60 feet (18.3 m) in front of her. In a few seconds she would be in motion. She would hurtle herself toward the vaulting table and do a roundoff onto the springboard in front of it. That would send her

McKayla Maroney flies through the air while vaulting during the team final at the 2012 Olympic Games.

BACKWARD

To most people, the idea of going onto the vault table backward seems crazy. Soviet gymnast Natalia Yurchenko was not one of them. She competed during the early 1980s. Before then, gymnasts launched themselves at the vault while facing forward. Yurchenko used a roundoff onto the springboard. It gave her incredible backward momentum. That allowed her to flip and twist more easily off the vault. It was not long before gymnasts all over the world were learning "the Yurchenko." Today it is the base for the Amanar and many other vaults.

shooting backward and upside down toward the vault. When her hands hit the table, she would push off and flip through the air. Her body would twist two and a half times. Then she would have to land on her feet.

That was the plan, anyway. Maroney's complicated vault was called an Amanar. It was the most daring gymnastics skill being done at the Olympic Games. The Amanar was so hard that only six women in the competition were trying it. Of those six, everyone agreed that nobody could do it quite like Maroney. After all, she was the defending world champion in the event.

"She has the best two and a half that anybody does in the whole world," said Martha Karolyi, the US National Team Coordinator.

Maroney was usually calm during competitions. But she was a little nervous about performing the Amanar in the most important competition of her life. The vault has a "blind" landing. That means the gymnast is not able to see the ground before her feet land. So if Maroney did not complete the twist in time, she risked injury.

Aliya Mustafina, a world champion gymnast from Russia, had badly injured her knee landing the Amanar the year before. Just before the London Games began, Maroney had hurt her leg and toe. She had not been able to train as much as she would have liked for her big Olympic moment.

But the moment had arrived all the same. The United States was fighting for gold in the Olympic team final. Vault was their first event. And Maroney was the last of her teammates to go. A well-done Amanar would

McKayla Maroney approaches the vault table backward during the event final at the 2012 Olympic Games.

set the Americans up for the next three events. But if she fell or even took a big step forward, the team would lose points.

Maroney took a deep breath and stepped into position. Her approach was flawless, with excellent speed and a smooth roundoff onto the springboard. And as she flew through the air she could sense that she was doing a very good vault. She landed as softly and effortlessly as a butterfly on a leaf, not moving. Maroney had stuck the landing.

Around the arena, the crowd erupted in applause and cheers. The vault was so well done that even the judges sitting off to the side were left

McKayla Maroney's stellar vault during the 2012 Olympic team competition put Team USA in good position to win the gold medal.

open-mouthed in amazement. Maroney skipped off the mat and into the arms of her coach and teammates. She knew she had done her job.

Vaulting to Success

Hands down, the Amanar vault was the most important skill done in women's gymnastics at the 2012 Olympic Games. No single skill in women's gymnastics is more challenging. The gymnasts who could do it received a difficulty score of 6.5 (since 2013 they get 6.3). That was more than half a point higher than almost every other vault done in the competition. That gave those gymnasts (and their teams) a big advantage.

Vaulting is the quickest event in women's gymnastics. From beginning to end, a gymnast's vault lasts less than 10 seconds, but a lot happens in that time.

WHY AN AMANAR?

The Amanar vault is named after Romanian gymnast Simona Amanar. She was the gold medalist on vault from the 1996 Olympic Games. Her final competition was at the 2000 Games. There she became the first woman to do a Yurchenko vault with two and a half twists. Amanar actually did not do the risky vault very well. It probably cost her a medal in the Olympic event final. All the same, it landed her in gymnastics' history books. That is because gymnastics skills are named after the gymnast who performs the skill for the first time at a major event such as the Olympics.

The gymnast starts at the end of the vaulting runway and runs toward the table, hitting the springboard with all of her force. That lifts her into the air and helps propel her over the table. During the second part of the vault, she flies through the air away from the table and lands on her feet.

Beginners start by learning simple vaults. As they progress, they might add an extra flip or twist. The most complicated vaults, like Maroney's Amanar, involve multiple flips and a lot of twisting.

In most competitions, gymnasts do only one vault. But in the event finals at major meets, gymnasts are required to show two different vaults to prove how they've mastered the event. Therefore, they will vault twice.

McKayla Maroney keeps her knees close and her toes pointed as she nears the end of her vault at the 2012 Olympic event final.

Quick Tip: Yurchenko Progressions

No gymnast, even one as talented as McKayla Maroney, starts out doing Amanars. First they need to get comfortable. After all, they have to approach the vaulting table while flying backward upside down. It's not easy. One exercise is to work roundoff back handspring, back tucks onto an eight-inch (20 cm) mat. Your feet should land just in front of the mat and force you to lift a little higher to get your hands onto the mat to complete the back handspring. As you grow more comfortable with this, an additional eight-inch mat can be added. This increases the height of the obstacle to simulate the vaulting table.

Form is very important while vaulting. Judges look for a clean, tight twist done without the legs criss-crossing in midair. The legs should be straight. The knees should be together and toes pointed. Properly executing an Amanar is especially difficult. The gymnast should be completely extended flying through the air, not bent or piked at the waist.

A good "block," or push, off the vaulting table is important to any vault. It is particularly key for the Amanar. This is how a gymnast gets enough height to complete the skill. To get good block off the table, the gymnast must position her back handspring entry at just the right angle. Maroney's Amanar is so good partly because she gets phenomenal block off the table. That leads to more height and time to complete her twist.

Floor Exercise with Aly Raisman

The softly simmering sounds of a violin were Aly Raisman's cue that this was it. Raisman was the last American to perform in the 2012 Olympic team final. Her floor exercise routine was the only thing standing between the United States and its first Olympic team medal in 16 years.

In one second Raisman stood at one end of the mat. Five seconds later she was at the other end. In between she had performed a blink-and-you'll-miss-it series of flips and twists. It ended with a flourish. She threw her arms in the air. The full house inside London's North Greenwich Arena cheered. The cheer was gentle, though. That is because Raisman's

Aly Raisman performs on the floor exercise during the women's team final at the 2012 Olympic Games.

WE ALL FALL DOWN

Falling is a part of gymnastics. That is especially true when it comes to learning new skills. When asked the secret to her success, 2009 world floor champion Beth Tweddle of Great Britain remarked, "It's just a lot of numbers and a lot of splatting before I get it correct."

routine was not yet over. She had completed one tumbling pass. She still had three to go.

Raisman had spent three years on the senior national team. That helped her develop into a top gymnast. At age 18 she was the oldest female gymnast on the US Olympic team. However, she had never been a superstar like Shawn Johnson or Nastia Liukin. Instead she was known for being very steady on every event.

Floor was the event where she truly stood out, though. Her explosive power allowed her to make the most complicated tumbling passes look easy. Three of Raisman's four passes included double saltos. Those are skills where the gymnast flips twice in the air before landing on the ground. She could crank them out like a machine.

"She's incredible," marveled gymnastics legend Mary Lou Retton. "She's such an explosive, exciting gymnast to watch."

Raisman's second tumbling run was called an Arabian double front. It was very rare for a woman to perform that pass. Once again, she launched herself across the floor. Raisman performed a roundoff, a back handspring, and then, as she rose into the air, a half twist followed by two front saltos in the pike position. She came down to a soft landing. Two down.

The United States had narrowly missed a team gold medal at the 2008 Olympic Games. The US gymnasts had been waiting for a chance to try again in 2012. And on this magical night in London, everyone had risen to the occasion. With every move Raisman made, another gold medal became more certain.

Aly Raisman flips through the air during the 2012 Olympic floor exercise finals in London.

Yet there was always an "if." In team finals, three gymnasts perform on each event. Everyone's score counts toward the team total. The Americans were well aware that one big mistake, or one injury, could be the difference between the gold medal and no medal at all.

But Raisman was concentrating hard. She had prepared too long for the moment to let herself make a mistake now. On her third pass, she hit a nearly perfect triple twist. It brought some members of the crowd to their feet, awaiting her final run.

Raisman did not hesitate. She hit a double pike salto on her final pass. And she landed on her feet in perfect time to spring upward into a jump. As she moved into her final pose, tears were welling up in her eyes.

From left, Jordyn Wieber, Gabby Douglas, McKayla Maroney, Aly Raisman, and Kyla Ross won the Olympic team gold medal in 2012.

She knew she had assured the Americans the team gold for the first time in 16 years.

"We knew we could do it," she said afterward, beaming, with the heavy Olympic gold medal on a purple ribbon hanging around her neck. "We just had to pull out all the stops."

Fun on the Floor

The women's exercise is the only gymnastics event done to music, and it's often a fan favorite. In order to be good on floor, gymnasts must master two things: a series of acrobatic elements that can be put together to create tumbling passes, and dance skills such as leaps and turns. Routines can be up to 90 seconds long, and a gymnast must perform throughout.

Young gymnasts must master basic tumbling skills, including handsprings, walkovers, and simple saltos. Then they can begin practicing more difficult flips and twists. Salto skills, where a gymnast completes a

DIFFERENT DOUBLES

The double back salto is the easiest form of double salto. Once a gymnast has mastered it, there are all kinds of complicated variations that can be learned. Double saltos can be done forward and backward. They can also be done in the tucked, piked, or layout (body completely stretched) positions. The layout is the hardest. Many top gymnasts also add twists to their double saltos. The most difficult variation to be tried so far is the double twisting double layout. This is when the gymnast cranks one full twist on each flip of her double layout.

flip without touching her hands to the floor, are among the first things gymnasts learn.

At the 2012 Olympic Games, Raisman performed several double salto skills. Double saltos can be done both forward and backward, but they are most often done backward.

Because of their difficulty, double salto skills impress the audience and judges alike. The gymnast who does several cleanly in her floor routine

Aly Raisman put together several great tumbling passes during her 2012 Olympic gold-medal-winning floor exercise routine.

Quick Tip: Doubling Up

Before a gymnast can safely perform a double salto skill, her body and mind must get used to the idea of flipping twice. Coach Al Fong has a nifty drill for gymnasts beginning to work double back saltos. The gymnast stands on a cheese-shaped mat stacked on top of a larger mat in front of a trampoline. Standing on the cheese mat, the gymnast bounces onto the trampoline and rebounds backward. Then she performs a back flip with an extra quarter salto, landing on her back on the cheese. "I love this drill," says Canadian coach Rick McCharles. "It's safe. Easy. Fun. And encourages good technique."

will usually earn a higher difficulty score than a gymnast who mainly relies on twisting elements when she tumbles.

A good double salto will have all the trademarks of good form. A gymnast's legs should be glued together. Sometimes the legs should be straight. This is if the skill is being done in the piked position. Other times the legs should be in a tight tuck. This is if the skill is being done in the tucked position.

Some gymnasts tend to do double saltos with their legs apart. This is known as a "cowboy" position. However, it usually results in a deduction. Good toepoint is also a must, even when rotating at high speed upside down.

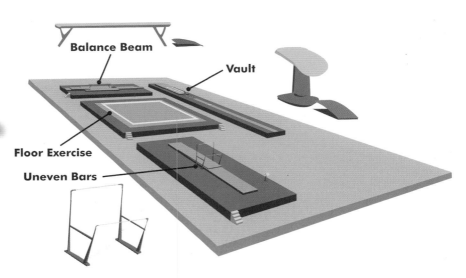

Balance Beam

Vault

Floor Exercise

Uneven Bars

balance beam

The balance beam tests a gymnast's balancing abilities, but also her nerve. Just four inches (10 cm) wide and four feet (1.22 m) off the ground, it can feel much higher when a gymnast is standing on it and thinking about doing a flip!

floor exercise

The floor exercise mat is 40 feet (12.2 m) long and 40 feet wide, with springs underneath a carpeted surface, allowing gymnasts to get more height on their tumbling passes, leaps, and jumps. Women's floor exercise is performed to music.

uneven bars

No event has changed more over the years than uneven bars. The bars were once closer together, but today they are set wider apart so the gymnast has more room to swing and do big skills.

vault

The vault runway is about 60 feet (18.3 m) long and leads to a springboard in front of a leather-covered vaulting table. The vaulting table replaced the narrower vaulting "horse" in international competition in 2001.

acrobatic
 Gymnastics moves such as handsprings and flips that are not
 dance elements.

block
 The push off the vaulting table that launches the gymnast into the
 afterflight of her vault.

conditioning
 Exercises such as pull-ups and push-ups that help a gymnast
 become stronger.

dismount
 The last acrobatic move in a routine. On bars and beam, the gymnast
 dismounts off the apparatus and lands on a mat.

pike
 A position where a gymnast keeps her legs straight but bends forward
 at the torso.

rotation
 A part of a gymnastics meet. At a competition, gymnasts do their
 first routine during the first rotation, the second during the second
 rotation, and so on. "Rotating" means moving from one event
 to another.

salto
 A flip, done forward or backward.

straddle
 A position where the gymnast points her legs in opposite directions as
 though she were doing middle splits.

stuck landing
 When a gymnast lands a dismount or tumbling pass and doesn't have
 to move her feet.

tumbling/tumbling pass
 A sequence of acrobatic skills done on floor or beam involving
 handsprings, flips, and/or twists.

Selected Bibliography

Graves, Will. "'Fierce Five' soar their way into Olympic history." *2012 AP Summer Games*. Associated Press. 1 Aug. 2012. Web. 5 Jan. 2013.

Graves, Will. "Sore foot forces world vault champ to take it easy." *2012 AP Summer Games*. Associated Press. 24 July 2012. Web. 1 Dec. 2012.

Macur, Juliet. "Golden Triumph Forged by a Friendship." *The New York Times*. The New York Times. 15 Aug. 2008. Web. 20 Dec. 2012.

Further Readings

Douglas, Gabrielle, and Michelle Burford. *Gold, Grace and Glory: My Leap of Faith*. Grand Rapids, MI: Zondervan, 2012.

Johnson, Shawn, with Nancy French. *Winning Balance: What I've Learned So Far About Love, Faith, and Living Your Dreams*. Carol Stream, IL: Tyndale Momentum, 2012.

Simkins, Kate. *I Want to be a Gymnast*. New York: DK Publishing, 2006.

Web Links

To learn more about gymnastics, visit ABDO Publishing Company online at **www.abdopublishing.com**. Web sites about gymnastics are featured on our Book Links page. These links are routinely monitored and updated to provide the most current information available.

Places to Visit

International Gymnastics Hall of Fame
Science Museum Oklahoma
2100 NE 52nd Street
Oklahoma City, OK 73111
(800) 532-7652
www.ighof.com
www.sciencemuseumok.org/gymnastics.html

Located inside Science Museum Oklahoma, the International Gymnastics Hall of Fame honors those who have had amazing achievements within the sport or contributed to the sport's growth. The hall of fame features collections that show the history of the sport and highlight the best gymnasts through memorabilia, videos, and photos.

US Olympic Training Center
One Olympic Plaza
Colorado Springs, CO 80909
(888) 659-8687
www.teamusa.org

The US Olympic Training Center in Colorado Springs is home to several elite athletes, including gymnasts, who are training for future Olympic Games. Tours of the complex are available.

ABOUT THE AUTHOR

Blythe Lawrence fell in love with gymnastics when she was eight years old, after watching the 1992 Olympic Games and reading Jill Krementz's *A Very Young Gymnast*. She has written about gymnastics for Universal Sports, espnW, the *Seattle Times*, and Examiner.com. Lawrence lives in Seattle, and would like to dedicate this book to her family.